W9-AFF-406

MEET THE VET/
CONOCE A LOS VETERINARIOS

By Joyce Jeffries   Traducción al español: Eduardo Alamán

Gareth Stevens
Publishing

Please visit our website, www.garethstevens.com. For a free color catalog of all our high-quality books, call toll free 1-800-542-2595 or fax 1-877-542-2596.

Library of Congress Cataloging-in-Publication Data

Jeffries, Joyce.
Meet the vet = Conoce a los veterinarios / by Joyce Jeffries.
    p. cm. — (People around town = Gente de mi ciudad)
Parallel title: Conoce a los veterinarios.
In English and Spanish.
Includes index.
ISBN 978-1-4339-9474-6 (library binding)
1. Veterinarians—Juvenile literature. 2. Veterinary medicine—Juvenile literature. 3. Occupations—Juvenile literature.
I. Jeffries, Joyce. II. Title.
SF756.J44 2013
636.089—dc23
First Edition

Published in 2014 by
Gareth Stevens Publishing
111 East 14th Street, Suite 349
New York, NY 10003

Copyright © 2014 Gareth Stevens Publishing

Editor: Ryan Nagelhout
Designer: Nicholas Domiano

Photo credits: Cover, pp. 1 Comstock/Thinkstock.com; pp. 5, 11, 15 iStockphoto/Thinkstock.com; p. 7 GK Hart/Vikki Hart/Taxi/Getty Images; p. 9 pixshots/Shutterstock.com; p. 13 Maggie 1/Shutterstock.com; p. 17 Digital Vision/ Thinkstock.com; p. 19 Monkey Business/Thinkstock.com; p. 21 John Wood Photography/Stock Image/Getty Images; p. 23 Hemera/Thinkstock.com; p. 24 (Horse, Airplane, Bird) iStockphoto/Thinkstock.com.

Printed in the United States of America

CPSIA compliance information: Batch #CS13GS: For further information contact Gareth Stevens, New York, New York at 1-800-542-2595.

Contents

Pet Helper 4

Animals in Need 8

Horsing Around 20

Words to Know 24

Index 24

- -

Contenido

Al cuidado de las mascotas 4

Animales en problemas 8

A caballo 20

Palabras que debes saber 24

Índice 24

Vets help animals!

¡Los veterinarios
ayudan a los animales!

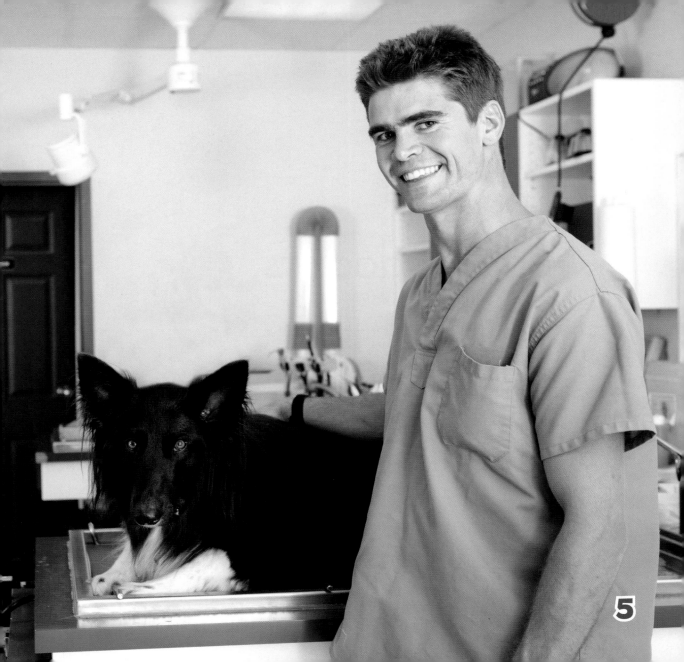

They are
animal doctors.

Son médicos
de animales.

They can give pets
things to feel better.
This is called medicine.

Pueden dar
medicamentos a los
animales. Así los
ayudan a sentirse
mejor.

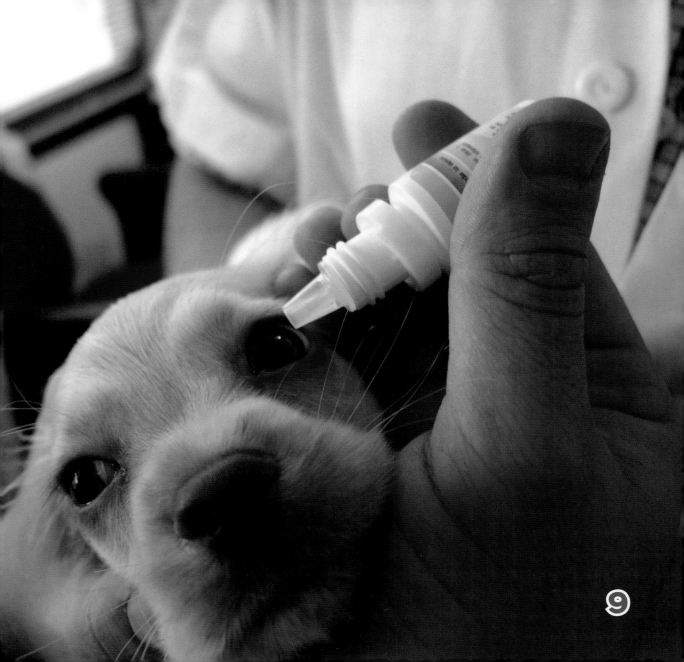

They fix a cat's paw.

Curan las garras
a los gatos.

They clean
a dog's teeth!

¡Limpian los dientes
de los perros!

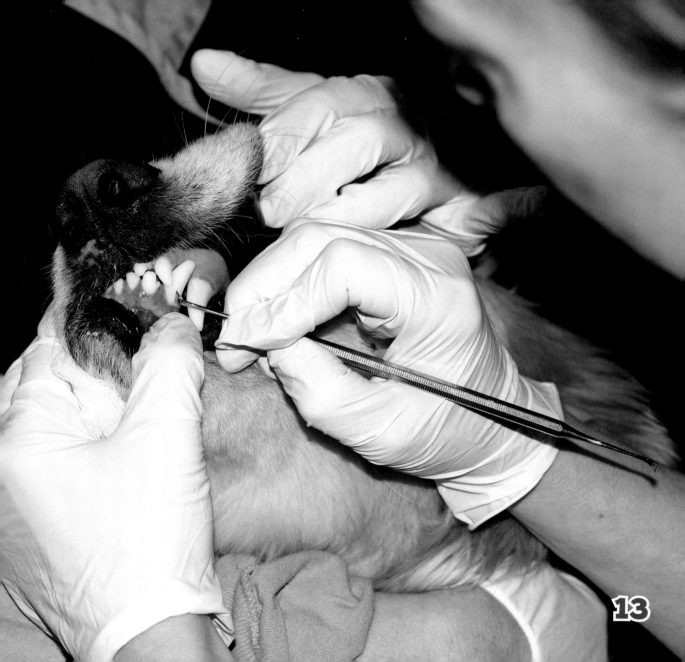

13

They set a bird's broken wing.

Los veterinarios curan las alas rotas de las aves.

Most vets work
in their own office.

La mayoría de los
veterinarios trabajan
en su propia oficina.

They visit farms to help sick cows and sheep.

En las granjas ayudan a las vacas y a las ovejas enfermas.

Some work with horses.
These are called
equine veterinarians.

Algunos trabajan
con caballos.

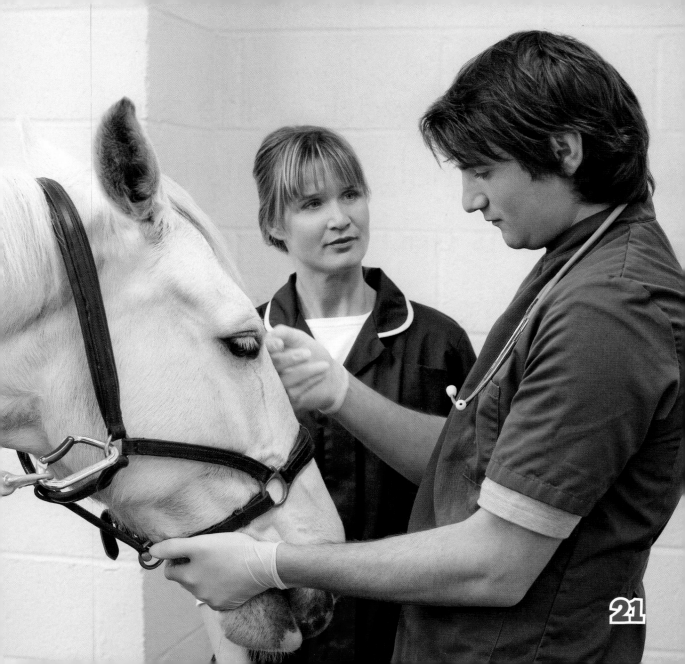

Others work at the zoo! They help big cats like lions and tigers.

¡Otros trabajan en los zoológicos! Curan grandes felinos como los leones y los tigres.

Words to Know/
Palabras que debes saber

horse /
(el) caballo

medicine / (el)
medicamento

wing /
(el) ala

Index / Índice

animal doctors/
(los) médicos de
animales 6

farms/(las) granjas 18

medicine/
(el) medicamento 8

zoo/(el) zoológico 22

24